Journey Transformed
Opening My Eyes to God's Truth and Grace

Juanita V Copley

Illustrated by
Valerie Beeman

Journey Transformed
Copyright 2020 Juanita V Copley
Illustrated by Valerie Beeman

Name: Juanita V Copley
Title: Journey Transformed; Opening My Eyes to God's Truth and Grace/ by Juanita V Copley
LCCN: Applied for
ISBN: 978-1-952369-43-8
Subjects: 1. Religion/General
2. Religion 012170 Christian Living /Personal Memoir
3. Religion 012040 Christian Living / Inspirational

Published by EA Books Publishing, a division of Living Parables of Central Florida, Inc. a 501c3

EABooksPublishing.com

I dedicate *Journey Transformed* to the family who has traveled with me during most of this journey—

Aimee, my daughter, my true soulmate who always understands God's gift to me

Devin, my son-in-law, a Christian man of integrity and love

Ford, my oldest grandson, a thinker and questioner who continually challenges me to be an authentic Christian

Cooper, my middle grandson, an optimist who never loses energy or a zest for learning…and soccer and country music

Tucker, my youngest grandson, a sweet, loving boy who always expresses his love for me with hugs and smiles

Valerie, Virginia, and John, my sisters and brother, who have always supported and loved me each in their own unique way

Journey Transformed

Opening My Eyes to God's Grace and Truth

Open my eyes, that I may see
Glimpses of truth Thou hast for me;
Place in my hands the wonderful key
That shall unclasp and set me free

Open my ears, that I may hear
Voices of truth Thou sendest clear;
And while the wave notes fall on my ear,
Everything false will disappear

Open my mind, that I may read
More of Thy love in word and deed;
What shall I fear while yet Thou dost lead?
Only for light from Thee I plead.

Open my mouth, and let me bear,
Gladly the warm truth everywhere;
Open my heart and let me prepare
Love with Thy children thus to share

Silently now I wait for Thee,
Ready my God, Thy will to see,
Open my heart, illumine me,
Spirit divine![i]

Table of Contents

Acknowledgements

Special thanks to my sister Valerie for listening to my stories and creating these lovely sketches to represent my journey transformations.

Introduction

"Attention! Attention! United Flight 245 for Chicago O'Hare is canceled due to mechanical issues. Please check with the United Representative for alternative reservations."

I slammed my computer shut.

"I just can't believe this! A fourth cancellation?" I shouted to anyone who appeared to be listening.

"That's United for you. I try to never fly them."

"You better hurry to the United help desk. They will run out of seats with all these cancellations."

"No one really cares, lady. We all are trying to get to Chicago."

Finally, the elderly lady sitting a few seats away smiled, "It will be ok dear, just go to the counter at gate 45 and they will help you."

"Thank you, but you just don't understand. I have wasted six hours of my time...six hours…waiting!" I packed up my bags, collected my partially eaten snacks, and stormed off to the reservation counter muttering, "Six hours…I have wasted six hours…six hours."

I was on a weeklong journey from Houston to the East Coast to the Midwest and then home…

a total of six mathematics presentations, eight dinners with mathematics supervisors, and countless interactions with prospective buyers. I was tired. And I was sick of people. Most important, I had purposely scheduled a day with my daughter in Chicago when I arrived, and now I wasn't sure I could even get there.

After another hour had passed, I was assigned to the last seat on an airline I had never heard of—Kiwi Airlines. I quickly prepared to board the plane, and in the process, I made a silent covenant. I would not talk with anyone. If possible, I would sleep and calm down. When we finally boarded the plane at 10 p.m., all rows were completely filled, with the exception of my row—not just one empty seat but a whole row of three for me to stretch out. Thank you, God! I certainly deserved all three seats. I spread my bags under the seats in front of me, sat in the aisle seat, and anticipated spreading myself out as well.

Then it happened.

Right before the door closed one more passenger came aboard. She was a beautiful, yet clearly distressed, woman holding more bags than she should have on a plane, and I knew my excitement was short-lived. She struggled to her window seat, moved my bags, hit me with one of hers, sat down and then she invaded my covenant of silence.

"So, why are you going to Chicago?"

"I'm going to see my daughter who's a student at college."

"Where?"

"A small Christian university you probably never heard of. Olivet Nazarene University."

"I know Nazarene. In fact, there was only one man who ever made a positive difference in my life, and that man was a Nazarene minister. I went to his church when I lived in Chicago." She paused, looked out the window, and then said "I was happy then, at least for a short time. But now, my life is a total catastrophe. In fact, I've just left my home and job in New Jersey. I am going to see my family one last time, before I..." Her voice stopped as tears streamed down her face.

Not sure how to respond, I gave her a tissue, and quietly said, "My dad was a Nazarene minister. He passed away a few years ago at age fifty-six. In fact, he pastored Chicago First Church of the Nazarene for only eighteen months many years ago. Who was your pastor?"

"Bill Varian."

Tears now suddenly streamed down my face. "That was *my dad*!"

For the next four hours on a darkened, quiet plane, Jesus came and sat in the middle seat between two ladies—one from Houston and one from New Jersey—in a God-anointed appointment about a pastor father who lived in Chicago. In the presence of God Almighty, we talked, shared experiences, prayed, cried, and prayed some more.

When we arrived and stood to leave the plane, a little lady in the row in front of us, turned around and said, "Hallelujah! God visited all of us tonight!" She was right. I have a feeling that many people on that plane heard our conversation. We parted as changed people. God interrupted our journey in an unexpected way, and together we experienced the grace, mercy, and love of God. We were never the

same again!

My Journey

Journeys come in different forms. Some are long; some are short. Some have detours; some are straightforward. Some are traveled alone; some have companions. Some are goal-focused; others are randomly selected. Some are intentional; others appear to have no purpose. Some are easily described; some difficult to understand. Some follow a specific path; others waver because of numerous obstacles. Some seem static; others are constantly moving.

In *Journey Transformed,* I have chosen to illustrate my different journeys through themes, rather than describe a chronological order of my life events. Many of my experiences, like the plane ride, were unexpected and not according to my plans. I have been rightfully called a control addict, and I admit that I am obsessive about calendars and planning. I faithfully complete five- and ten-year calendars with

7

specific goals outlined for each year, a more detailed yearly calendar, monthly calendars with specific times described on each day of the month, and my daily to-do list that contains events every thirty minutes. However, I continue to learn that (1) I can choose my responses to life events, (2) I can depend on a God incarnate who has created and understands me, and (3) God is in the business of transforming my life into His image with His grace and truth.

My journey has been interrupted by unexpected events many times, some good and some bad. Reflecting on the events, I can say that with God's grace and truth, I have experienced far more good than I had ever expected.

- FROM the unfaithfulness of a spouse and resulting divorce TO a beautiful marriage of thirty-six years to the love of my life.

- FROM poverty as a single mom TO a life of unbelievable blessings, including money and so much more.
- FROM cancer, radiation, and chemo for my husband and my four-year-old grandson TO an understanding of illness and hurts, as well as the tender arms of a loving God and healer.
- FROM publishing buyouts with loss of contracts TO new opportunities that have resulted in travels all over the world, presentations in thirty-six states, and a multitude of educational and writing opportunities.
- FROM teaching layoffs and job lost TO a life of jobs in universities, Washington DC, Hollywood, and more work in retirement than I ever could do.

- FROM the premature birth of a daughter with many health issues TO a daughter co-pastoring with her husband, with three boys, currently serving God in a mission field in the United States.

- FROM the death and loss of my beloved husband, my precious parents, and many close friends TO an understanding of grief combined with new perspectives and yearnings for a heavenly home.

In *The Wisdom of Tenderness,* Brennan Manning states,

> "We must be ready to allow ourselves to be interrupted by God. It is a strange fact that Christians and even ministers frequently consider their work so important and urgent that they will allow nothing to disturb them. It is part of the discipline of humility that we must not spare our hand where it can perform service and that we do not assume that our schedule is our own to

manage but allow it to be arranged by God." [ii]

God's truth has helped me see my life journey through the eyes of an "eternal picture." Rather than dwell on events that I don't understand or attempt to help God see *my* plan, I think about my life as a continuous journey and how God's purposes can be accomplished through me with an eternal perspective. My favorite verses from Proverbs 3:5–6 (KJV) remind me of God's grace and truth.

"Trust in the Lord with all thy heart." (He has never forgotten me.)

"And lean not unto thine own understanding." (Yes, God has helped me increase my understanding. However, my knowledge is inadequate to face all my experiences.)

"In all thy ways acknowledge Him." (My Creator, the One who couldn't love me more or less no matter what I do.)

"And He will direct your path." (Sometimes through silence when He expects me to do what I know to do, sometimes through open or closed doors, sometimes with a direct word, and sometimes with an unexpected experience.)

As you read the chapters in this book, I pray that you will think of the events in your life that may be part of your journey. I have no doubts that you can think of other or bigger journey ideas as you consider the transformative events that occur in your life. My prayer is that you too will reflect on these events, the choices you make, God's truth that you hear, the gift of God's grace that you receive—and the resulting transformation you can experience as you walk this journey. Let's start walking!

Chapter 1

The Beginning

"What a perfect life!"

I am a preacher's kid, a PK. When I was born, my father was a beginning pastor who had just graduated from Eastern Nazarene College. As the son in a struggling, working-class family, he had worked his way through school with a variety of jobs, a charismatic personality, a love of sports, and a devotion to God and God's calling on his life. From all accounts, my father grew up as the main support—financially, emotionally and spiritually—for his family. My mother's background was quite different. A recent college graduate with a teaching degree in biology, she was known as the quiet twin, pretty,

intelligent, and "the perfect preacher's wife." Her
father was a successful contractor who came through
Ellis Island from Ireland at the age of seventeen and
put his brothers through college before marrying the
love of his life, an Englishwoman. My mother was
nurtured in a home of love and acceptance and lived
in beautiful houses built by her father.

My parents had been married for eighteen
months when I entered the family, a healthy baby girl
with a lot of hair who resembled "a baby monkey,"
obviously a precursor to my great beauty as an adult!
My earliest memories are of princess-like dresses,
curly hair with bows, and confidence that I was the
very pretty, smart daughter of my perfect father and
mother. Two sisters and one brother were born over
the next twelve years, but they soon discovered—and
I frequently proclaimed—that I was the "oldest and
boss" of them all.

As often occurs in PK families, I viewed my father as my version of God. I knew he was perfect. After all. he told us what God said every Sunday. My earliest memory was when God and my dad healed my hands. I had burned my hands badly on an open oven door, after which black scabs covered my hands. I wondered if they would ever look pink again. After several days and many prayers, my dad, a.k.a. God, peeled off the scabs, and I was amazed at the miracle of my new pink hands.

My dad frequently told me how much he loved me and how proud he was of me. Of course, that attribute was God-like, and when paired with the message that I could do or be anything I wanted to be, it became my image of God. I translated it to goals of my own. I decided I would be a perfect daughter! Initially, my goals were to get all A's every school year, read every book in our small town library, obey all ten commandments (happily, I didn't need to worry about the adultery one), memorize more Scripture verses than anyone else at Bible school, be a first-chair flutist in both band and orchestra, win every spelling bee in Southeast Elementary School, get a job as early as possible, and be someone really important in life. I wanted him to be proud of me, and I thought that if I reached for perfection, God would be proud of me too.

Amazingly, I remember my first forays into imperfection in great detail. In kindergarten, I broke the ninth commandment by lying three times. Specifically, I told Dave Barton that I needed crayons because I wanted him to sit by me, I told my mom that I had a good day in kindergarten when my teacher Mrs. Stipe corrected me because I talked too much, and I told my dad I was in bed when I wasn't. My first B+ was an 89 in the first semester of eighth grade science from Mrs. Young. I looked in the mirror at age twelve and counted exactly 123 pimples on my face, crying at my very imperfect skin. I got in trouble when I answered the phone and told a parishioner that my dad was playing golf on Monday and further explaining that he just needed rest from all the church people who were always bothering him. I felt guilty because I fell asleep in my closet rather than praying for an hour like the evangelist had said we were supposed to do. I got into big trouble when I interrupted an important board meeting to exclaim that I had just fallen on my *butt* while ice skating with all the church kids. That was "not appropriate language for a young lady." In third grade, I was the first person to sit down in the spring spelling bee because I spelled *sandwich* incorrectly. In sixth grade I cut the nose off my wooden paddle four times in shop class, and my apron project never did have a straight hem. When I broke my finger playing basketball with the boys, I lost my place in the orchestra and missed the state competition, which in the words of my orchestra director, "disappointed the whole school." I could go on and on.

One event further illustrates my beginning journey. I began my sophomore high school year in a new school and tried out for the fall school play. When I received the lead in *Death Takes a Holiday,* I was so excited. My family invited many relatives and friends to the opening night, and they were in the front rows cheering me on. I performed well, and when the curtain closed, I realized my father was not in the audience. I discovered that he was furious at the moral of the play and blamed the teacher and me for not recognizing that the true love "that casts out all fear" was not the love of the characters in the play, but rather the love of God. He told my director and me how disappointed he was in both of us. I was so embarrassed, and although he allowed me to finish the performances, I was reluctant to perform again in plays. I wanted my classmates, my teacher, and especially my dad to see how perfect I had been—but instead, my dad, a.k.a. God, was extremely disappointed.

Why is this rather comical and somewhat sad list of imperfections important to my story? Simple: I have searched for perfection most, if not all, of my life. Do I remember when I accomplished a goal? Yes, but not in detail and normally not as a celebration. Instead, even at a young age, I remembered and reenacted my imperfections over and over again. Yes, my beginning life was almost perfect. I had a wonderful mom and dad who provided me a home of love, joy, and righteousness; two sisters and a brother who were my best friends; a loving, supportive group of mentors and teachers; a good education, a healthy environment, and many advantages. Yet despite all my beginning advantages, my goals of continual perfection could have derailed my journey.

I have spent much of my academic life researching mathematics motivation in young learners. In motivational learning research, a condition called "learned helplessness" occurs when children or adults primarily focus on their performance for others rather than on actual learning. These strongly performance-oriented people typically underestimate their successes and overestimate their failures. Perfectionism is more prevalent among females. People can become negative about life and learning, and when this situation occurs over time, they can become "learned helpless," give up easily, and make little effort. My perfectionism placed me on a path to learned helplessness.

In her book, *The Gifts of Imperfection,* Brene Brown states definitions of perfectionism that describe a self-destructive and addictive belief system and result in feelings of shame, judgment, and blame. She advises that we should "embrace our imperfections" and that in this process, we will find "courage, compassion, and connection," essential attributes if we are to let go of perfectionism and work on becoming ourselves. [1]

One of the scriptures I memorized early was from the Sermon on the Mount, and it became my mantra early in life: "You therefore must be perfect, as your heavenly Father is perfect" (Matthew 5:48 ESV). Taken out of context and interpreted as perfection in all things, this command is impossible. I have found that God's truth, as often proclaimed in the written Word and by His servants, has taught me that in this statement Jesus is summarizing his high ideal of perfect love, i.e., love God and love your neighbor. His truth and grace along with His amazing love has given me examples of the type of love this verse implies, a love of others and even my enemies. I am thankful that through God's grace and truth, I am learning a new perspective on perfection.

As you read this book, you will see that I still reach for perfection in all I do. You will also observe that I acknowledge my vulnerabilities to shame, judgment, and blame. I hope you will see that the perfection of demonstrating God's love to both others and myself is a process involving courage, compassion, and connection—a transformation not yet complete in me. Thank God that I continue to mature in that love.

Chapter 2

A Journey with Passion

"I just *love* teaching!"

It was the most unusual audience. I had recently retired from the University of Houston, and my husband and I decided to take a trip to mission fields in Poland that we had supported, cruise around Italy, and take a side trip to Bulgaria to visit some friends. While we were in Bulgaria, I was invited to speak to teachers who taught in an orphanage for Roma students. As soon as I entered the doors, both teachers and students warmly greeted me with smiles and verbal greetings that I didn't understand.

The students were unlike any I had ever met. My guide told me that the children at the orphanage were Roma, often known by the derogatory name

"gypsies," a traditionally itinerant ethnic group,
lacking educational opportunities, and often facing
discrimination. Also, each of the students in the
orphanage had a disability of some type. In Roma
culture a disability meant they were cursed and that if
anyone touched them, they too would be cursed. Most
of the students lived in the orphanage because their
families had disowned them. As I greeted each child
individually, I intentionally shook their hands, and
many of the students reciprocated with hugs.
Although I could not understand their verbal language
as they showed me their work, I had no doubts they
felt loved. They in turn loved and respected their
teachers.

In a similar way, the teachers demonstrated
their love and respect for their students. It was
obvious that they weren't worried about curses or
disabilities. Instead, they showed me their students'

work, the posters they had created with the Cyrillic alphabet, and their meager teaching materials. They bragged about the students who had broken away from Roma stigmas. Their passion about teaching, caring for, and loving their students was daunting, and I felt totally inadequate to talk to them about teaching. Instead, I listened to them through an interpreter, encouraged them by telling them what I had observed in their classrooms, and gave them some materials they could use in their teaching. I prayed for them, that they would continue to show God's love to His children.

This experience in Bulgaria is one that I will never forget because it reminded me of the reason I was a teacher and my lifelong journey with passion. Passion can be defined as a deep, abiding love for a person, place, or thing. I do have a deep love of teaching, but it involves so much more than just the act of teaching. It involves the students who learn, whose lives are changed by what they have learned. It involves listening with respect as students teach me about how they learn. It involves thinking of new ways to help every student learn. It involves motivating learners to think, to help others learn, and to better be able to function in the world. Passion is when I wake up in the morning with thoughts of teaching, or students, or new ways to motivate them to learn. It is more than just enthusiasm, excitement, or a job. As much as is possible, I have put my heart, mind, and soul into teaching, and I have been privileged to be on this lifelong journey with passion.

From the very beginning, I wanted to do "something important" for God and others. And I didn't want to be bored. As a college freshman, I majored in mathematics, and thought I would do technology and mathematics and work in the financial world. I didn't think teaching was for me, because "everybody did that" and I wanted to do "something really important." At the end of my freshman year, I became an assistant to the mathematics professor who taught a required math class for prospective elementary teachers. As part of my duties, I taught review sessions for the students who had difficulty with math. I found that I loved it, and I was good at it. In fact, I reviewed so well, that the professor thought I had cheated because everyone passed the course with an A or a B, something that normally did not happen. After lots of prayer and consultations with advisors, I changed my major to education with an emphasis in math and science. My passion for teaching was just beginning.

I have been teaching in educational settings for fifty years. From that early beginning in my sophomore year until today, I have been privileged to teach in full or part-time positions in Chicago, Illinois; Kansas City, Missouri; many different schools in Michigan; and more than forty schools in Houston, Texas. I have conducted workshops or presentations in forty-eight of the fifty states and internationally in Bulgaria, Poland, Japan, Spain, Bermuda, Australia, and Indonesia. I have worked on hundreds of curriculum projects and grants, specifically with National Head Start in Washington, DC, *Curious George* in Hollywood, and *Mister Roger's Neighborhood* in Philadelphia. I have taught high school, middle school, elementary students, early childhood students, graduate students at all levels, and inservice and preservice teachers. Have I been bored? Absolutely not. Have I been able to follow my passion? Yes. I loved going to work (most days), I couldn't stop thinking about ways I could help students learn, and according to my family, I said yes to teaching opportunities more than I should have.

But my big question is: Have I been able to do "something important" for God and others? Teaching math and instructing teachers how to teach math has been my primary focus, but at the beginning of my journey, I wondered if God could use math to accomplish something important for Him and others. I knew I wasn't a pastor, a missionary, or a leader in a church organization. I also knew that I was always given opportunities to teach in public schools and universities rather than church-related schools. Most importantly, I knew that my life was dedicated to God, He had created me, knew my strengths and weaknesses, and He had directed me on this journey. I have faith I serve a God who knows me, cares about my passions, and smiles every time I experience the joy of teaching. With His direction, I have learned so much during this passion journey. Let me describe several of my most important discoveries.

Early in my career at the University of Houston, I was given the opportunity to teach in Jakarta for a month during the summer. Many of the teachers or administrators who worked in their schools had been my graduate students, and we had worked on the national curriculum together. Naturally, I was thrilled to do a series of lectures and presentations for the teachers, as well as their students in the primary schools.

My graduate students had assured me that all the methods I had taught them in their university classes would work in Indonesia and that they had all the technology I would need to make presentations. So, I packed up my stuff. I knew exactly what I was going to do. After all, I had a doctorate in education, I had given many lectures, and I knew precisely what each presentation should look like. I was ready.

Unfortunately, I was totally unprepared. First of all, the climate was even warmer than Houston, and I had packed only skirts (good), light blouses (mostly good *if* I had a jacket), and sandals (not good). I learned that sandals made me look like a servant, and no one would listen to a servant tell them how to teach. Okay, I would buy a pair of comfortable shoes at the store. But I was a giant in Indonesia. I couldn't find any shoes my size, so instead I wore the only pair of heels I had to every teaching assignment. *Ugh!*

Second, although they had all the technology I needed, they normally did not have electricity. My computer, with wonderful graphics, videos, and presentations could not be used at all. Of course, with little or no electricity, we had no lights, and even poster displays did not show up. So I taught with just my words and physical actions, although with Franz as my interpreter, I am not sure what was said.

Third, I didn't have enough of the materials I needed to teach. I never dreamed that more than a hundred teachers would stand and listen to me talk with an interpreter for more than two hours in 100+ degree temperatures after they had taught all day. So later I went to the local market and bought some materials that could be adapted for my presentations. I learned so much, and I freely admit that my presentations at the end of the month were much better than those at the beginning.

What was my important discovery? Simply put, effective teaching was much more than thorough preparation—as in my perfectionist-planning obsession from chapter one. In Jakarta, I had to learn as I taught and exhibit great flexibility and adaptation.

More importantly, there were many God-effects to my teaching, events I did not expect. My graduate students in Indonesia knew I was a Christian. Some of them were also Christian; most were Muslim or Buddhist. While the graduate students were in Houston, my husband and I had picked them up for church on Sundays. Those Sunday visits became so popular that many of the Muslim believers joined us for services and lunch as well. We had many interesting discussions about the meaning of communion, the turkey meat that looked like ham, why we celebrated Easter with chickens and bunnies, and the excitement of the American car wash. In Jakarta for a month, the Christians welcomed me to their churches every Sunday—some government sponsored, some not—and the memories of their joyful worship services still are imprinted in my mind.

A second teaching discovery occurred after I had officially retired from teaching. A few days before Thanksgiving I was dreading the grocery store, crowded lines, shopping cart traffic jams, and the food bill at the end. I was only fixing dinner for seven people, but I still needed lots of groceries, so I braved the crowds. I hadn't left myself enough time to complete this task and risked being late for a conference call that I had to attend. My inner mantra was, "Focus, focus. Pay attention to your list. One row at a time. Don't miss something. You don't have time to go back and forth. Focus, focus."

As I rounded the corner of an aisle, I witnessed a shopping cart crash. One woman with a completely full cart tried to pass another woman with a small cart containing just a few items. The cart of the passer hit the other cart and smashed the finger of the one passed. "You should not be going so slow!"

the passer shouted as she indignantly strutted by. "Can't you see we are all in a hurry?" Tears ran down the cheeks of the one passed as she clasped her finger and stood there as if she were glued to the floor.

I went to her to find out how she was and if she needed help. Her bruised finger was not the issue. After a brief introduction, she explained her hurt. "This is my first Thanksgiving without my daughter. She was killed this year. . . She was only sixteen, and I am having a hard time doing anything." There in aisle 13, I listened to Tiffany's story, told her about the God of all comfort, and prayed for her. What a marvelous opportunity to teach a lady who needed to hear that God loved her!

The next day I returned to that same grocery store. Yes, I had missed the ingredients for the cranberry sauce I was supposed to get the day before. As I rushed toward the checkout lane, I heard another crash, saw a partially turned-over display, and heard two young voices arguing.

"There's Ms. Nita! Let's go see her!"

"No, I don't think it's her. She's just disguised as Ms. Nita. She lives at church!"

I smiled, got out of line, rescued the display, and revealed to them that indeed I was Ms. Nita. As so often happens with young children, Elijah and Evelyn assumed that because they only saw me in Junior Church, that was where I lived. After a brief discussion, Evelyn explained to her younger brother, "Ms. Nita eats too! She even goes to the grocery store!"

What did I discover about the importance of my passion for teaching in these two experiences? It doesn't matter if I am retired from a teaching career. I am a teacher, and it is impossible to quit teaching and say when and where I teach. In both cases, I was in a grocery store. For Tiffany, I was a disciple of Christ, listening, comforting, and praying with her. For Elijah and Evelyn, I was not "in disguise" but rather a normal person, not the delegate from God who taught them about Jesus on Sunday. As a teacher and a disciple of Christ, I have the opportunity to teach everywhere and all of the time, whether by word, attitude, or action. And it needs to be positive, not negative.

The most important discovery I have made overshadows all others and is one I consider every day. If I am to be an effective teacher, I must focus on my students, their cognitive abilities and understandings, their emotional needs, their physical issues, and their attitudes about learning. I listen to them because I respect their ideas and their perspective. I observe them because I strive to understand their motivations, I challenge them to be persistent because I know that effort is the primary indicator of learning, and I expect them to be the best at whatever they do. I have found that my passion is constantly fueled when I can teach with my eyes opened to students, prepared to learn *from* them as well as to teach *for* them. Curriculum is essential, yes. Flexibility is critical, yes. Objectives that connect to practice are crucial, yes. Preparation is necessary, yes. Communication skills are helpful, yes. However, as I reflect on my teaching episodes, I know that when I focus only on *what* I am teaching rather than *who* I am teaching, I miss the chance for excellence. This discovery is also abundantly clear in a few student stories.

Quiet Jessica was one of my sixth grade students during my early years of teaching. At the end of the year, I asked each child in my class to give me a report card for being a teacher, a dangerous requirement for middle school students *and* for their teacher. I stressed the fact that they should tell me good things as well as things I could improve. Jessica took my directions seriously and wrote:

> Ms Copley You were real good
> with the dumd kids. They needed you
> and you halped them. You were real
> good with smart kids. You always
> keeped them buzy, but you should do
> better with the plane kids like me. I
> need to learn to! Luv, Jessica

Jessica taught me that I needed to understand that all students. Even the "plain" ones needed my help and had the right to learn.

Tucker, my excited nine-year-old grandson, was reflecting on the lesson I taught in Junior Church from Psalms 23:1. Everyone in his small group had memorized "The LORD is my shepherd; I shall not want" and from my perspective, I had done an excellent job describing the meaning of "I shall not want." When I asked him about the lesson, he said, "I just got it, Meme, but not until the very end. I thought it meant I don't want the Lord to be my shepherd, and I didn't know why you thought it was good that we were sheep. I was so messed up. I think you should pay attention to the period after the word shepherd so that kids will see they are two different things." I am so glad I listened to Tucker; I just wish I had heard his misunderstanding earlier. Although I had explained the verse by describing wants and needs and God's provisions, his question was different. What did I learn from Tucker? Something that I have learned and relearned many times: listen to students' questions and then address their questions and any misunderstandings. If I don't listen, I won't know.

Betty had been teaching third grade for twenty years in the same school system. I met her when her principal "strongly recommended" that she learn from me how to teach mathematics. In return, she strongly responded that she did not need my help, that she knew how to teach third grade math, that the principal didn't like her, and that the standards-based math curriculum was not necessary for nine-year-olds. Simply put, I was not welcome to be her teacher. After listening to Betty's concerns, I realized that we needed to address Betty's needs in small steps. I chose a new math concept, understanding decimal numbers for third grade, taught it in Betty's class every day for thirty minutes, and discovered that Betty's understanding about mathematics grew as well. After just one month of observing, encouraging, teaching, and reflecting, her students all passed the test, and her principal began bragging about Betty's work. In return, Betty wanted to share all of this new information with the other teachers on her team. I suddenly had a new friend, and when Betty was asked to be the team leader in math the next year, she invited me to share my expertise. My passion was spreading!

What did Betty teach me? She showed me that I could learn from reluctant, negative students. Her initial reaction was hurtful, and I admit I wanted to ask the principal for another, more positive student. Instead, I listened to Betty daily—and learned—as she reflected on my lessons, observed as she learned, encouraged her as she worked with her students, suggested that she share her new expertise, and most importantly, helped her develop her own leadership qualities. I can't say that Betty became passionate about teaching decimals. But I can say that her attitude about teaching mathematics became more positive *and* she confidently shared her expertise with her peers.

So how has my journey with passion been transformed? I thank God daily that He directed my life to the world of teaching. Initially, I did not have a passion or even an inclination to teach; my choice was quite different. However, as I learned the skills necessary for effective teaching and began to focus on the needs and abilities of students, I became more and more passionate about that role. I *love* teaching. And I am glad God "worked all things together" in my life so that I can travel this journey with passion.

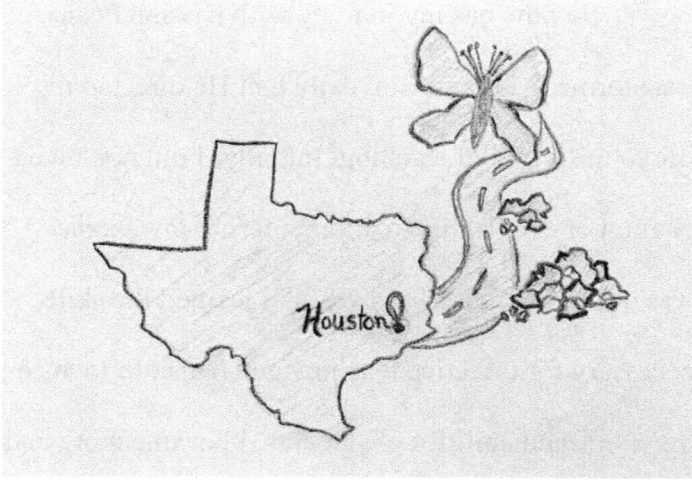

Chapter 3

A Journey of Obedience

"Houston, Texas... alone?"

February 12, 1976. I was seven months pregnant, assigned to bed rest, miserable, and trying my best to fix a dinner for my husband and his parents. When everyone was finished eating, I stood and announced that I was going to bed and I hoped someone could clean up for me. From the other room, I heard the complaints. "She is always so selfish! It's as if no one has ever been pregnant before. Certainly she could stay with us for a few minutes at least." But that night I just didn't care what anyone thought. I closed my eyes, feeling so alone and questioning how I could go through another two months of bed rest in this small Kansas City apartment.

49

When I awoke the next morning, everyone was gone. My phone rang, and my father shouted, "God told me to call you. How are you feeling? What's your blood pressure? Call the doctor!" Although I felt as if I were moving in slow motion, I took my blood pressure and discovered it was at a dangerous level. At my father's insistence, I called the doctor and was told to go to the hospital immediately. I don't remember how I got there, but when I arrived I was quickly diagnosed with toxemia, poked with needles, and placed in an operating room.

I will never forget the words of Glen Haswell, my wonderful Christian doctor. "God and I have this, Nita. Let's pray. It's too early to bring your baby into the world, but our tests show that we need to so that both of you will live." As we prayed, peace surrounded my soul. I knew God would take care of both of us. When we finished praying, I asked if my baby could be born the next day. That way my baby would be born on Valentine's Day rather than on Friday, the thirteenth of February. Dr. Haswell laughed, and said, "Sorry, she will be born in about thirty minutes. Get ready, honey. When you open your eyes, you will be a momma."

Aimee Marie was born on February 13, 1976. She weighed in at four pounds, two ounces and dropped to three pounds after a few days. Her right lung was diagnosed with hyaline membrane disease, making it difficult for her to breathe. She was placed in an incubator where she could receive the care she needed. Because I was in the intensive-care unit on another floor, I did not see her for several days. When they finally rolled me up to the neonatal unit, I remember looking through the glass at this little body breathing in short, quick spurts, with tubes coming out all over her body. Only skin and bones with big, gleaming eyes. Certainly, she didn't look like the baby I had expected, but it made no difference to me. I turned to everyone and exclaimed, "Isn't she just beautiful?" And she was! Although she had some early health issues, Aimee Marie came home after six weeks weighing five pounds, a precious gift from God.

After the birth of Aimee, the next three years were difficult. My husband graduated from seminary, and we moved from Kansas City to Michigan, where he pastored a church and I taught school. While pastoring, he confessed to multiple affairs and theft, and he spent several months in a Christian mental health facility, where he was diagnosed as manic depressive and bipolar. While he was in the hospital, I moved to a different city, bought a house trailer, and began teaching in a new school district. With medicine and counseling, my husband lived with us for a year until his behavior became dangerous to Aimee and me. I filed for divorce in 1979.

I began questioning God's role in my life. I thought I had obeyed God and done everything I was supposed to do. I had committed my life to God, I went to church, I prayed for His direction, I tithed, I worked hard, I loved my husband, I witnessed to many people about God, I graduated from a Christian college, I supported my husband through seminary, I obeyed every commandment, and my list continued on and on. I certainly knew I wasn't perfect. However, I just thought that if I did what I was supposed to do in my life, if I obeyed God's laws, everything would turn out wonderfully. Now I wondered what I had done wrong. Was God mad at me? Did He care? What did He want me to do? Why did this happen to me?

Christmas 1979 was my first as a single mom. I sat on the sofa in my house trailer, pondering the crooked Christmas tree, the two presents under the tree, and wondering how I was going to get through this season. I didn't want to call a Christian friend or a member of my family. I didn't want to read the Scripture. And I certainly didn't want to listen to any sermons or Bible study lessons. I had been trying to hold it together for my three-year-old, but now that she was in bed, my tears flowed. Feeling alone and unloved, I succumbed to my own personal pity party.

Then the doorbell rang. When I opened the door, Santa Claus greeted me with a smile. "Is this the home of Aimee and Nita? I brought some presents early because I will be too busy on Christmas Eve."

I invited him in and called Aimee to get up. "Santa's here! Santa's here!"

Aimee climbed out of bed, gave Santa the once over, and said, "Mommy, don't be so excited. I knew he was coming. You told me!"

Santa then emptied his bags of forty wrapped presents—twenty for Nita and twenty for Aimee.

After Santa left, I ignored all of my motherly instincts and both of us opened *all* the presents selected especially for us. None of them had the name of the giver (they were from Santa, of course), but they all were given "with love and prayers." I had no doubt that they were from my friends at church, the friends who loved and supported us during that very difficult year.

Before Santa Claus knocked on the door, I had been focused on me, on my situation. In my self-pity bubble, I was unable to think about God's blessings or even read the Scripture or listen to advice from Christian friends. My focus on self and negative comparisons with others resulted in self-pity and defeat and a heart that was not open to God's truth and grace.

Certainly, the "Santa Claus" evidence touched my heart; however, I continued to have more questions regarding obedience and God's direction in my life. In early February 1980, I was pink-slipped from my teaching job in Michigan, my sole source of income. I prayed for God's guidance, and in case He had forgotten, I frequently reminded Him that I had previously obeyed Him. I read and reread many Bible verses that talked about God's care and guidance. Psalms 121:8, "The LORD will keep your going out and your coming in from this time forth and forevermore (AMPC)." And Isaiah 41:10, "Fear not, for I am with you; be not dismayed, for I am your God; I will strengthen you, I will help you, I will uphold you with my righteous right hand (ESV)."

My prayers (and some of my questions) were answered with an open door that I know was directed by God. My brother had recently graduated and was beginning a new job in Houston, Texas, a city that I heard needed teachers. In late February, I interviewed in six school districts in Houston and was offered jobs in all of them. Because I believed that I was obeying God's direction, I quickly accepted a teaching job in Houston and made plans to begin a new life in a large city with a very precocious three-year-old.

Those who loved me did not easily accept my decision. In his typical style, my father had found me another teaching job in Michigan, had plans for converting their basement into an apartment for Aimee and me, and had even found and purchased the perfect car for me. He could not believe that I was going to "godless Houston" and taking his only grandchild more than 1200 miles away from him. My church friends even offered to open a private school with me as the director if I would stay in Michigan. Other friends found a teaching job that was "perfect for me" in the Upper Peninsula of Michigan because they were sure "God wanted me *in* Michigan." It was clear to me that I would be leaving my strong support system by going to Houston. As I prepared to leave, I felt alone and totally responsible for Aimee's well-being and care.

Our belongings were packed into a small Jartran trailer and primarily consisted of Aimee's toys and my books. I didn't know how to back up a car with an attached trailer, so I often had to enlist the help of strangers to park appropriately. I had only 300 dollars to buy furniture for our apartment, and my "new" furniture consisted of a mattress bought on the side of the road, an awful plaid chair and couch complete with cigarette holes, and a metal table-and-chairs patio set. Our apartment was small, close to my school, in a rough place of town, and importantly, the best one I could afford. With my teaching salary and no other income, child-care, gas, and living expenses, we had thirty dollars left for food and laundry expenses each week.

Sound difficult? Yes. Did I question my decision? Sometimes. Did I feel alone? Yes. But God's presence continued to show evidence that He was there. Was I really obeying God when I went to Houston? Most days I thought so. Did God really direct my path? Initially, I hoped so. Now, more than forty years later, I can say, absolutely! I learned so much about myself, God, and His grace and truth in those first years in Houston.

My journey of obedience has been transformed over the past forty years. While I listen to the perspectives of others and think seriously about my own plans, I focus on God's guidance and discovering what His Word proclaims. While I often want an easy path, I realize that often the most difficult acts of obedience result in surprising opportunities and experiences. While I evaluate the results of my decisions, I acknowledge that there are many things I don't need to understand. While I still consider what others say I *should do,* I now think more about what I *could do* and remain excited about the possibilities for my future. I constantly remind myself and sometimes others that I am in charge of simply obeying God, and He is in charge of the results.

Chapter 4

A Journey with Loss and Failure

"God can… but if not?"

On a hot summer day in July, the garbage collectors at the Coldwater City Junkyard viewed an interesting, albeit strange demonstration. To symbolize the death of my first marriage, I went to the city dump with my wedding dress, my wedding photo album, and a large plant that was given to us to celebrate our sixth anniversary. Standing on the top of a mound of garbage, through tears and shouts, I cut and ripped my dress to shreds, I tore the pictures to pieces, and I broke and pulled the plant apart. As I wreaked destruction on each item, I cast the pieces all over the pile. At the end of my hour-long destruction, I shouted, "Yes! It is finished!" And then, for the first time, I noticed the group of workers who had gathered to observe "a very crazy lady." They were

63

smiling, and I returned their smile with a rather embarrassed nod and a quick thumbs up.

I had never considered divorce to be an option in my life. My minister husband and I were married in a large church wedding, supported by my family and friends, and I believed that our promises of commitment even "in sickness and health" would always be part of our journey. However, his diagnosed mental condition, refusal to take the needed medicine and therapy, and his dangerous behavior necessitated that I file for divorce. In my view, one that my husband repeated as well, the person who knew the most about me no longer loved me. I was a failure at marriage.

My husband's initial mental breakdown was very public—and all over town. He was a minister of a growing church, I was a teacher in the local public school, and we were viewed as a young, successful, caring couple. So the members and friends of the church were devastated by our failure and did not understand the actions of their pastor. Nor did I. While he was in the hospital, I remained the healthy one who handled the normal life challenges, the completion of my teaching contract, a move to another city, a new teaching assignment, weekly visits to the hospital, paying the bills, and most important, performing the role of mother to two-year-old Aimee. Unfortunately, most of the church members blamed me for his mental condition. The lady who watched Aimee while I was working refused to continue; church members accused me of stealing curtains from the parsonage; and they entered our home when I was at work to monitor our move. Letters, verbal statements, and their actions as I moved out of the parsonage were crushing to me. I had prayed with and for these people, I had worshiped with them, I had visited them when they were sick, I had led many of them to Christ—and yet they were mad at me. How could they? Why couldn't they see this situation as I see it? I became bitter.

My family provided a great deal of support for me during this time of loss. Aimee and I lived with them on the weekends, and her grandparents, aunts, and uncle played with her, influenced her music choices (Uncle John's "Hey, you, get off of my cloud" and "I can't get no satisfaction" were her favorite lyrics and *not* mine), and together they demonstrated the love and happiness we both needed. We attended church with them on Sundays, and one particular Sunday evening we attended a healing service. The minister asked those who needed a special touch of healing to come to the altar for prayer. I felt compelled to go to the altar to be healed from my bitter spirit. When the minister prayed, a surge of peace surrounded my soul, and at that moment I knew my bitterness had been given to God. My transformation had begun.

Almost a year later, my newly organized life crashed and radically changed. That week more than just the weather was cold and overcast. I had just been pink-slipped from my teaching position; I had formally filed for divorce from my husband of seven years; my new school had recently been burned by a disgruntled employee, destroying many of my teaching materials; and the bills were too high for me to move away from the trailer park. On Monday I sat in the hospital, waiting for the doctor to tell me if they were going to do surgery on my three-year-old daughter for the blockage in her lungs. Not a good way to start the week.

The week did not improve. It got worse. Although I was not at fault, I was in a car/pedestrian accident in which I hit a small boy who happened to be the son of the chief of police. Fortunately for all of us, the young boy was not seriously hurt, but I spent hours reliving the details of the accident with a variety of witness reports. My bills were rapidly increasing, my daughter was admitted to the hospital for surgery, and those closest to me were supporting me with lots of advice and answers–as long as I did what they suggested. I felt alone and totally defeated.

By the following Sunday my life still had not improved. I went to church only because I always did, and I didn't know how I would explain to my sweet daughter that I didn't feel like going or that I was mad at God and very afraid that He had left me forever. But I went. I sang the familiar songs, bowed my head when we prayed, listened to the sermon stoically, and didn't speak to anyone. I couldn't! At the end of the service, I went to the altar and knelt. I did not cry or pray a passionate or religious prayer. Instead I said something like this, "Dear God, *if* you are there and you care about me, please know this. You do *not* need to do anything else in my life or even answer one of my prayers. You do *not* need to provide for me or help me feel good. You do *not* need to bless my life. That is up to you. I just want You to know that I will always serve You because you are God. I don't need to understand what You do or don't do. You made me and I am your child." I rose from the altar with no feeling or tears, but in that moment, I had recommitted my life, my purpose, and my joy. At that altar, I did something very important. I acknowledged that my life was God's *not* because of what He does for me, but because He is God. I was saying that I didn't need to understand and I didn't even need to feel His presence, that whatever I felt, whatever I questioned, I believe in a God who loves me and cares for me. My life was His.

As a child, one of my favorite stories in the Old Testament was the story of the three Hebrew boys and the fiery furnace (Daniel 3:16–18). When they were ordered to bow down to King Nebuchadnezzar, they responded,

> We do not need to defend ourselves
> before you in this matter. If we are
> thrown into the blazing furnace, the
> God we serve is able to deliver us from
> it, and he will deliver us from Your
> Majesty's hand. But even if he does
> not we want you to know, Your
> Majesty, that we will not serve your
> gods or worship the image of gold you
> have set up. (NIV)

When I pray I frequently repeat those three words, "but if not," (Daniel 3:18a, KJV) especially in times of loss or failure. Like most people, I have had many experiences of failure and loss. Some have been failures in my professional life as a university professor: rejection letters for articles or books for publication, promotion denials, non-funded grants, or poor presentation reviews. Others have been failures in my work as a teacher: students whom I have ignored and whom I have not been able to help, ineffective or poor planning decisions, and teachers whom I have not mentored well. Many losses have involved personal relationships: friendships lost due to misunderstandings, conflicts of opinion, loss of respect for boundaries, and conversations that were thoughtless or impulsive. Still other losses are more personal: unfulfilled health goals, imbalanced priorities, and poor financial decisions. Whatever the case, I believe in a personal God who cares for me especially in times of failure or loss.

One of the hardest losses is the death of someone close to you. In December 1985, my father had a heart attack at the age of fifty-six and died two days later. At the time he was serving as an evangelist in the Church of the Nazarene, and because of his ability to communicate the good news of the gospel with integrity and authenticity, he was well known and respected. As the oldest child, I felt responsible to help my mother adapt to her new situation, so I shelved my grief and concentrated on the many details that had to be handled with the death of her spouse, my father.

Because of a grant I had received, I was fortunate to meet most of the astronauts on the space shuttle *Challenger.* In January 1986, a month after my father's death, I had all my students watch the *Challenger's* televised epic launch. And it exploded, right on TV, in front of me and my class of first graders. My sudden grief over the loss of the astronauts and the lingering grief over the loss of my father melded together to overwhelm me. I will forever remember being surrounded and comforted by six-year-old children, who with words and pats told me it would "be okay."

I had difficulty understanding the reasons my dad died at such an early age, and I often questioned God's plan for our family. I reminded God that He had healed another evangelist who frequently preached with my dad. Why didn't he heal mine? Didn't God know that my mom and my brother and sisters needed my dad? Didn't God know that people still needed to hear more of God's Word? Didn't God know that I needed my dad's guidance and love? At those questioning times, I was again reminded of the three Hebrew boys' words, "But if not . . . ." And I remembered my commitment to God.

I have no doubt that God answers my prayers, sometimes with a resounding *yes*! And the blessings are obvious to all. Other times His answer is a quiet *yes*, and I don't realize the blessing until much later. I think of it as a blessing disguised. Still others are *wait* or *no*, and I acknowledge that He knows best. Indeed, He has answered my prayers; just not in the way I wanted. I have also learned that loss and failures are part of life, and it is often in those moments that I draw closer to Him. God has richly blessed me, healed my bitter spirit, met all my needs, and taught me so many lessons. He has showered me with His grace and mercy over and over again, and I am thankful for His presence, especially on my journey through loss and failure.

Chapter 5

A Journey of Forgiveness

"I cannot forget. But now…"

It was my third Sunday in a new church. I had recently moved to Texas as a single mom with my four-year-old daughter, and I traveled across town to a church that was similar to the one I attended as a child. After attending an adult Sunday school class, I entered the sanctuary to worship. The woman who was serving as a greeter walked up to me, introduced herself and said, "I just heard that you are divorced and that your husband was a minister. I am so sorry that you are no longer a Christian. I am praying for you!" Then after the worship service, one of the assistant pastors mentioned that my daughter could get a scholarship to a children's camp because she was aware that we had a "broken home" and that the scholarships were for children who did not have two parents who were Christians. I left church that day totally discouraged and dismayed.

Because my beliefs mirrored the ones generally supported by this particular church, I continued to attend Bible studies and worship services there. But I ignored many programs specifically designed for divorced people or people with broken homes. I was not often invited to be involved in the activities for couples, nor was I invited to teach any Bible classes even after I volunteered. I was isolated from my Christian community because of my labels: "divorced" and "broken home."

The judgments continued. Years later when I brought a male friend to church, I was warned, "Be careful. Marriage should not be to someone who does not have the same background you have. The Bible says that you shouldn't be unequally yoked." Then when my spirited daughter was too loud, or "not ladylike," some friends volunteered to "work with her and help her" because I obviously didn't have time to be a "good mother." Those comments were especially hurtful because they weren't based on truth. At that time I was not even considering marriage to my male friend, and I was extremely proud of my spirited daughter and the way she had matured and developed.

Of course, not everyone in my church was judgmental, but it was easy for me to focus on the negative comments. For many years I have had difficulty forgiving my church friends for the labels and the resulting actions I received. I decided that I would only be involved with groups that accepted who I was, and I tried to forget the biases I experienced. As a Christian, I knew that I must forgive others, but I have often had difficulty forgetting the situations and those who unfairly judged and labeled me.

God has taught, and continues to teach, me the act of forgiveness. He has also revealed to me the judgments and labels that I have made of others. Even at an early age, I kept a tally of things my sisters and brother did that required forgiveness. (Like when my brother folded the legs of my favorite paper doll or my sister threw a shoe at me because I got up earlier than she did. How terrible!) My tally never reached the scriptural level of seven times seventy (Matthew 20:22) so I decided I had to sigh and forgive forever.

I had many experiences in Houston that required forgiveness. As a lead teacher in large school districts, I served as a Child Advocate and often represented the children who had been abused, ignored, or misdiagnosed. I often found it difficult to talk rationally with any adult who hurt a child, and yet, I constantly had to remember that God loved them and would offer them forgiveness. As the Chair of the Department of Curriculum and Instruction at the University of Houston, I was sometimes asked to *forgive* students who cheated on exams, *forgive* professors who were inappropriate with students, *forgive* students who missed graduation deadlines or *forgive* some office employees who failed to do their job. I found that I could have an attitude of forgiveness, but that there were still consequences that had to be faced. As a member of multiple church boards, I *forgave* the music pastor for his infidelities, a youth pastor for inappropriate behavior, and a Sunday School teacher for alcoholism. In all these situations, there were consequences that had to be faced. I only had to forgive.

In one situation someone I respected stole a large sum of money from our church. He faced the appropriate consequences and made plans to return the money. Although he never apologized and asked for my forgiveness, I knew that as a Christian, I had to forgive him. As I prayed, God reminded me of a situation that I faced when four-year-old Aimee and I were alone in Houston. We were at the grocery store and the cart was already full with our thirty dollars worth of groceries. By my calculations the bill would be just a bit over twenty-nine dollars, and I knew that I could not buy one more item. As we walked by the fruit section, Aimee saw the apples and said, "Oh Mommy, can I have just one? I really like them." For just a few minutes, I looked around at the area, checked the mirrors and realized that we were alone. I thought, "Who would see me? I could put it in my purse. Aimee needs to get something special. I want her to have it. It's just an apple! No one would know." I am very thankful that I did not steal the apple, but I certainly thought about it. God reminded me how easy it would have been to steal something for my child. Fortunately, His Spirit prompted me to do the right thing, and I listened and obeyed. This reminder of God's forgiveness and guidance helped me forgive my friend, and I had no doubts that God would forgive him as well if he asked.

The journey of forgiveness is a long one. After my husband's mental breakdown, I left the church parsonage with a great deal of bitterness. God healed me from that bitter spirit. But I often emphatically said I would never go back to the rural community where it had occurred. I wanted to forget all of their bad notes, comments, and actions as I left. Again, God had other plans.

After I retired from the University of Houston, I moved back to Michigan to be with family. Because I had served as a consultant for National

Head Start and the Department of Education, educators in the state department asked me to work on a regular basis with teachers in elementary and preschools. I set several guidelines for potential districts: the school leadership had to be supportive, and the districts needed to be located close to my home so that I could meet with teachers weekly. State leaders selected two specific districts, and they especially recommended one because it met my requirements and the teachers' specific needs.

God had a surprise for me. The recommended district was in the same rural community I had left more than thirty years previously, a place I never wanted to see again. Imagine my hesitation when I discovered that the schools I had to visit were on the same road where I had once lived. In fact, I went by the parsonage and the church twice a month for two years, and every time I drove by, God prompted me to pray for them. What a lesson in forgiveness! Every time I drove by the church, God reminded me of His blessings in spite of the disappointments there. He reminded me of His grace and mercy as He forgave me and that His forgiveness was for everyone who believed in Him.

God's Word continues to speak to my soul about forgiveness. In Isaiah 43, two words separate Israel's sinful past from their promising future: "But now." Let me paraphrase the message as it relates to me.

> *But now* this is what the LORD says . . . he who created you [Nita], he who formed you [Nita]: Do not fear for I have redeemed you; I have summoned you by name, [Nita] you are mine. When you pass through the waters [failures and loss], I will be with you; and when you pass through the rivers [false labels and words], they will not sweep over you. When you walk through the fire [absolutely anything harmful], you will not be burned; the flames will not set you ablaze. For I

am the LORD your God, the Holy One of Israel, your [Nita's] Savior. . . . Since you [Nita and everyone] are precious and honored in my sight, and because I love you [Nita], . . . Do not be afraid, for I am with you [Nita]. . . . See, I am doing a new thing! [I can forgive because I am forgiven!]. (Selected portions from Isaiah 43:1– 19, NIV)

Yes, God has done a new thing in my life through forgiveness of others, including myself. Indeed, forgiveness is a journey. I remember, *but now* I have forgiven others. I remember, *but now* I am forgiven. I praise God for His forgiveness!

Chapter 6

A Journey of Love

"Could I love again?"

"So when are we going to become a family?" six-year-old Aimee asked. She sighed loudly, sat back in her chair with her arms crossed, and waited for a response from Chet and me.

After what seemed like a very long silence, Chet looked at me and simply said, "What do you think?"

I thought it was a good idea. We finished our lunch and looked for a house that afternoon. We were engaged!

Romanic story? Not really. Who proposed marriage? Aimee. When did the big engagement event occur? During lunch after church on Sunday. How long had we been dating? Five months. Why did

Aimee propose? Because she knew Chet, "the man who really loves me," couldn't stay overnight unless we were married. Was it really love that would last? Yes—for all of us, Aimee, Chet, and me—an enduring love and a marriage that lasted for more than thirty-six years until his passing.

I first encountered Chet at a social gathering of 100–200 professionals who met once a month to discuss issues and provide opportunities to meet other single adults. For three months, Chet was in my small group, and all I knew about him was that he worked at a church. I assumed he was a minister, so I wasn't at all interested in knowing more about him. I certainly did not want to be involved with another minister, but I soon discovered that God had other ideas.

One night after the November gathering, Chet was standing alone, drinking a glass of punch and eating a cookie. Since I was waiting for my ride, I decided to find out more about him. "So you work at a church. Are you a pastor?"

He was not. He was the custodian of a church.

"Yea! You are a custodian!"

He smiled. "Thank you. I don't normally get that great reaction."

We had our first date later that week. While I was waiting for him to pick me up, I told my friend that from what I could tell, Chet was not who I thought I would like. He was a cowboy type; I was an academic. He only had a high-school education; I was working on my master's degree. He liked country western music; I liked classical music. I was sure he would pick me up in his truck, that he would be wearing cowboy boots, and that he would be dressed in western wear. I was wrong—partly. He was perfect for me! Yes, he drove a truck, he wore boots, he was dressed in a western jacket, and he loved country western music; however, I soon discovered that he was a kind, loving, intelligent, and godly man.

To me, marriage love involves three important elements—romance, friendship, and commitment. Fortunately, our marriage had all three. As our engagement story indicated, our romance was not the type normally visualized on movie screens. Chet never remembered Valentine's Day ("So, exactly why is Valentine's Day important?"). He never sent me flowers ("They just die!"). And he never led me around a dance floor, whispering sweet words in my ear ("Sorry, I just keep stepping on your feet"). With that said, we had a beautiful romance. Chet taught me that I could love again. He considered my feelings, respected me, patiently listened to my needs, and approached any issues with a sense of humor and confidence. I felt loved by his actions, his hugs, his smile, and his encouragement.

Two events in our early marriage illustrate the romance in our relationship. My father died a few years after our wedding. To help my mother, I traveled with her and returned home several days after Aimee and Chet did. When I walked in the door, Chet greeted me with a hug and a small package that contained a beautiful pearl ring, the engagement ring I never had. Knowing that Chet never spent money he didn't have and knowing that he didn't have any money, I wondered how this beautiful present was purchased. Aimee quickly informed me that they had gone to a pawnshop and Daddy had given them some old rings, his former wedding ring and a class ring and then got lots of money to spend on a ring for me. How romantic, a true gift when I especially needed it.

Another romantic, yet frightening, event illustrated the complete loving trust Chet and I had between us. Four years after our wedding, I was working during the summer term as a graduate assistant to complete my doctorate. I had an hour between classes and decided to call the blood bank to inquire why they wouldn't take my blood the day before, a blood donation I normally did every six months. After waiting for ten minutes, a nurse explained to me that my blood showed "borderline HIV," and that I needed to see my doctor as soon as possible. I quickly drove the sixty miles home, contacted Chet, and met him at the doctor's office for more testing and lots of very personal questions. I will never forget Chet's absolute trust in me and my absolute trust in him as we talked about our previous and current sexual experiences. After some investigations about my recent periodontal surgery, some more physical tests, and an agonizing week of waiting, the result was declared as inaccurate and the diagnosis was categorized as a mistake. Now I only remember the diagnosis as a romantic moment of trusting love.

Chet and I were also great friends. We simply loved being together, laughing, playing, exploring, celebrating, and even crying. Chet and I both worked hard and experienced many years of wondering how we could keep our heads above water as we paid for our home despite many foreclosures in our neighborhood, kept our car and truck working as we traveled hundreds of miles each week, took care of Aimee and her needs, and just lived. As we could afford it, we traveled a great deal. We especially enjoyed traveling to many countries, often on mission trips. Simply put, we found great joy in helping others. Sometimes we got on the wrong train, sometimes our flights were delayed, sometimes we got lost, sometimes we ran out of money, but we always enjoyed ourselves. We were so excited when our grandchildren arrived. Singing, playing games, and telling stories with the boys was truly one of the joys of our lives. We laughed often, played silly games, enjoyed eating with friends, and perhaps most importantly, prayed and worshiped God together. Chet was so proud of me and I was proud of him. He believed I could do anything I wanted and I believed the same about him. We were never disappointed in each other. Indeed, we were loving friends.

Commitment is the most important element of my loving journey. As already indicated by our engagement story, Chet was committed to both Aimee and me, and we were committed to him. *We* got married to Chet; *we* all got wedding presents; *we* had a party after the wedding; *we* all lived together in the same house; *we* ate together and shared everything. But only two of us went on the honeymoon!

A year after our wedding, Aimee asked Chet about having his name because she felt she was his "real" daughter. Chet was delighted, and we began exploring the necessary procedures. He got some extra work on the side so we could pay for the three lawyers needed to adopt a child. Thankfully, Aimee's birth father was happy for the adoption and he quickly agreed. The court date was on a Thursday morning, and Chet, Aimee, and I dressed up in our finest and arrived as soon as the door opened. Unfortunately, it was difficult to get all three lawyers there at the same time, so we waited in the family courtroom for more than three hours, watching families divorcing, spouses arguing before the judge, or men being incarcerated for not paying child support. Finally, our three lawyers arrived, and we were called to the front.

Picture petite seven-year-old Aimee standing in the center with Chet and me holding her hands and surrounded by three very important looking men with briefcases and reams of documents. The judge's bench was very high, and Chet and I could barely see him. Aimee could only hear his voice and the sound of rustling papers. At the judge's request, the lawyer for Aimee's birth father, Chet's lawyer, and the lawyer representing Aimee presented their information regarding the adoption using the necessary legal vocabulary. Then the judge spent five minutes reviewing Chet's commitment and responsibilities to Aimee. We all listened intently as Chet responded, "I understand and I will" to each of his new responsibilities.

Finally, when it was quiet and the procedure appeared to be over, a small voice rose from the center of our group, "Hey, isn't anybody going to ask me what I think?"

As we all chuckled, the judge stood and looked over the bench to see the little girl at the center of this legal contract, "Well, Miss Aimee, do you want this man to be your daddy?"

"Yes, sir! More than anything in the world!"

At that, the judge pounded the gavel and announced, "This is the best thing I have done all day! Aimee, meet your daddy. Chester, meet your daughter!"

The tears flowed, with smiles all around, and Aimee was officially adopted by Chet Copley, a man who taught me that love was romantic, and the best love involved friendship and a mutual respect. Most importantly, Chet understood and taught me that love was a commitment to a spouse, our child, and to the

God who lived within us.

Chapter 7

A Journey out of Control

"Kyrgyzstan? Where in the world is that?"

It was a typical Sunday night in Houston, Texas. Chet and I were sitting in our pew on the left side, halfway back from the front. The music had been inspirational, the testimonies had been good, and the pastor was finishing his sermon with a call to the altar to those who wished to pray. Rather than bowing in prayer, I was busy focusing on our fifteen-year-old daughter. Aimee had recently been promoted to the teen group and was seated down front on the right side of the church with her friends. I hoped she was paying attention and not talking or writing notes.

As I watched, she stood, walked slowly to the altar, and bowed to pray. I had no doubts that Aimee was a committed Christian. At an early age, she had prayed and asked Christ to be her Savior. I also knew that she often went to the altar to pray about specific requests for herself or her friends. However, this time was different. My heart sank. I whispered to Chet, "She has been called to be a preacher! I just know it." Why was I dismayed at the notion? Simply put, I did not want her to be a minister because of the experiences I had as a pastor's wife, a pastor's daughter, and especially the views that many people had about a woman in ministry. I didn't want *my* daughter to go through all of that. She was very talented, could do so many different things, and should do something else. Please God. Don't call her to be a preacher.

I have often been called a "control freak," a label that I have justifiably earned. Over the years, I have attempted to control my daily schedule, my students' pursuits and behaviors, my diet, our family's budget, my academic goals, my widowed mother, my husband (an impossibility), and even the weather conditions by preparing for every possible contingency. Since God had given me this beautiful daughter, I really wanted to control her decisions as well. I wanted her to use all of her gifts and avoid some of the difficulties that I had encountered. It made sense to me. Fortunately, God had a different plan for both Aimee and me.

After Aimee's initial commitment to be a minister, she had many experiences that both solidified her call and allowed her to ignore it. Our pastor gave her many opportunities to speak on Sunday evenings, she was involved in drama groups that witnessed to God's grace, and she often recited Scripture passages during worship services. She won awards at the national level in communication, enrolled in Olivet Nazarene University, served as Freshman Class President, accompanied and taught with me on a month-long trip to Indonesia, and graduated with honors as a secondary teacher with majors in English, History, and Communication. After her college graduation, I began to breathe easier. Perhaps she would forget her call to be a pastor. Or realize that she could be a wonderful Christian, be a gifted teacher, get married but not to a minister, and have my grandchildren. Control crazy I was. Fortunately, God had other plans.

One Wednesday night, Chet and I were sitting next to Aimee at a church prayer meeting when she again affirmed her commitment to God's plan. At the time, she was teaching middle school students in a low income, public school district, a position where she had experienced many successes, had her own apartment, and was very involved in the church's praise team and children's program. To my surprise, she stood and announced that at the end of the school year, she would be going to another country to serve as a volunteer missionary. She said, "I am twenty-four, and it is now time for me to follow God's call on my life."

As an effective controlling Mom, I smiled, but only outwardly, and said that of course I wanted her to do what God wanted, and then asked lots of practical questions. How will you pay for that? You have to be debt free to serve as a volunteer missionary. Can't you serve as a missionary teacher? Your students need you. Don't you need more details about where you are to go? What country will you go to? How do you know there is a job? Is it safe? Can't you serve God here in the United States? There are lots of needy people here, and you wouldn't need to learn another language. And most importantly, how can you leave your dad and me?

I soon learned that God and a committed Aimee are impossible to control. Within three months, Aimee had gotten an extra job as a server at a very popular restaurant, made enough money to travel and pay her debts, and had an invitation to serve as a missionary and a teacher in a third-world country. She made all the arrangements to store, sell, or pack everything she owned, obtain multiple visas, travel across two continents to Kyrgyzstan by herself on planes, trains, and cars, and arrive in Bishkek, the capital city, ready to teach missionary children. I was certainly not in control.

The day she left Intercontinental Airport in Houston was one of my saddest. Yes, I was proud of Aimee and her decision. Yes, I knew that God had worked it all out for her to go. Yes, I knew that many prayers surrounded her. Yes, I knew that we had dedicated her life to God when she was just a baby.

But could this possibly be God's plan? It certainly wasn't mine. Did she really know what could happen to her in a place I couldn't even pronounce? Was a Muslim country a good place for this strong, opinionated daughter? All alone? Surely, this could not be the right decision. I had absolutely no control over her actions, much less those of unknown others.

For the next eighteen months we communicated daily with Aimee via email, and we were able to hear her voice in a few shouting conversations through the internet, using the best means we had at the time, a kind of short-wave radio. We also were able to travel to Paris to visit my brother and his family, where she joined us for a week. I got in some of my control-based questions during that time, but mostly God helped me understand that she was right where she was supposed to be. She loved teaching the two girls of a missionary doctor, enjoyed the experience of teaching at the international school, learned Russian fluently enough to communicate or at least understand the language, shared Bibles with Muslim girls, was the English-speaking radio disc jockey at the local radio station, experienced cooking everything from scratch, and made many friends. Her love of people from any background or experience grew exponentially, as did her love for God. Yes, she had some difficult or frightening experiences, but fortunately, she did not share those with me until much later. I began to breathe easier and decided that God and Aimee had everything under His control. And given that her assignment in Kyrgyzstan was for two years, she only had six months to go.

On September 11, 2001, all of that changed.

Initially, I was not concerned about Aimee. Rather, I thought about my brother who had been in

110

New York the day before or was on a flight back to Paris. After a few hours and lots of news and rumors about the perpetrators of the attacks, I began investigating where Aimee was in relation to Taliban groups. What I discovered was quite alarming to this controlling mother. She was living in a border town close to a Taliban group who professed to hate Americans. When I contacted Aimee to tell her about the attack, she said that she had seen it on the computer, but that she was fine. "Mom, the *babushkas* love me here. There is no problem. I do not need to come home." I went into total control mode. I enlisted the help of everyone in authority in her sponsoring group, the missionaries she worked with, and family members who lived in Europe. I just knew that Aimee had to come home, and I did not exhibit much faith in God's power to do what I knew had to be done. I was *out of* control.

Aimee arrived home to Houston on October 1, 2001, six months earlier than expected. With God's grace and provision and lots of conversations, we were able to reflect on the past situation, and I was able to evaluate my need for control with some clarity. Aimee lived at home for a few months, substituted in her former school district, and served as a translator for Russian visitors to a local oil company. She did not forget her call to serve God and in January moved to Kansas City to enter the Master of Divinity program at Nazarene Theological Seminary.

The next few years were much calmer on my control journey. After all, Aimee was going to school in a Midwest town, working as a waitress to pay for her schooling, and meeting lots of other Christian friends. I thought that with a seminary degree, she could maybe serve in other roles like administration in a Christian college or mission, maybe even a professor, rather than a preacher. So I continued praying and asking questions, still trying to exhibit some control.

Again, God had other plans, and as always, His plans were perfect. While attending seminary, Aimee met Devin, a talented and committed Christian. Their personalities meshed perfectly, they loved and respected each other, and I had nothing to do with their meeting or relationship. They married, graduated from seminary, and began serving as co-pastors in the Church of the Nazarene—without my control. So now there are two preachers in my immediate family, not just one.

Although God has taught me many things, I have found that my control obsession has not totally stopped. One starry night God spoke directly to me. I was sitting by the window on a United flight traveling from Chicago to Houston, feeling overcome by a very difficult situation at Aimee and Devin's church, one that was unfair and untrue. I was looking out at the sky and yelling, inside of course, and accusing God of not taking care of them. I asked, "Don't You know they have been serving You? Don't You know they could do something else? Why aren't You changing the situation?" And I was also thinking, "If they had done some other job, or if I had been in control, it would be better."

As tears flowed down my face, God whispered, "Don't you know that I love them *more* than you could possibly love them? Don't you know that I have called them, and I will bless them? Nita, don't you know that they have put their lives in My hands, *not* yours?"

As in any ministry, there are both encouraging and discouraging experiences. Aimee and Devin have been privileged to serve in several churches as pastors. They have followed God's direction, and I have no doubts that God is using them as His servants. I have prayed for them daily, celebrated their successes and shared their burdens. For the past five years, my pastors have been Aimee and Devin Mulder. I am privileged to hear their sermons and their biblical knowledge, watch the many people they lead to God, pray with and for them, and learn from their commitment to God's leadership. I continue to try and control and prepare for the weather (very difficult in Michigan), my budget, my diet, my life, and even my grandkids (just a little). But God keeps reminding me that He loves me and He is in control.

Chapter 8

A Journey Infused with Joy

"Share more. . . Yes!"

On a cool, dreary day in late September, I stood on a small, weed-covered hill on the sidelines of a cross-country match as more than a hundred middle school students ran by. A small cluster in front had already passed, then another, and another. But I was searching for a very important person, my twelve-year-old grandson. Then I saw Ford. His countenance showed determination with just a bit of stress and effort. When he saw me, I got a slight smile, and he quickened his pace just a bit. As I shouted and cheered, I realized that tears were flowing down my face.

As I searched for a tissue, a fellow onlooker thought I was disappointed, and tried to provide some encouraging words, "He's in the middle group. There's a lot more coming. I am sure he will improve as the year goes on."

I wasn't crying because Ford was in the middle group. He had improved his time from the previous race. And it wasn't because I was sad. My tears were filled with joy. I was celebrating God's healing power as I remembered a picture of a very different Ford years earlier.

The phone call was one of those that you never want to hear. My daughter called to tell me that our four-year-old grandson, Ford, had woken up with bruises covering his body, and they were taking him to the doctor to see what could possibly be wrong. Immediately I thought of leukemia, and although I tried to be encouraging, my voice was shaky as I said

I would begin praying. Within a few hours, I received another phone call to tell me that Ford was being ambulanced to DeVos Children's Hospital, about forty miles from their home. I continued to pray, as did our wonderful church family. Throughout the afternoon and late into the evening, Ford's blood was tested over and over again. They tested his blood marrow to rule out leukemia. Our prayers increased, and we prayed specifically "Not leukemia!" After a blood marrow test, our prayer was answered as we requested—not leukemia! Instead, his condition was labeled as ITP or Idiopathic Thrombocytopenic Purpura. To this day, I remember my relief that it was not leukemia. As a teacher, I had had several young students die of leukemia while they were in my school. I knew what could happen, and it just couldn't happen to my oldest grandson. Surely God would know that. So I quickly prayed my praise to God and informed my church family of the wonderful answer.

Unfortunately, the new diagnosis did not relieve him of disease. ITP is an autoimmune bleeding disorder characterized by abnormally low levels of blood cells called platelets. It is caused by antibodies in the blood that attack the platelets. Ford's ITP was originally labeled as acute, a condition that normally stops spontaneously after three-to-six months. In Ford's case, however, it took two-and-a-half years. He experienced an illness that involved frequent blood draws, medicine typically prescribed for leprosy patients, steroids, ten chemo treatments, many doctor appointments, and bouts of anemia. He was very weak and several times had to be physically carried home from school or ride in a stroller designed for a toddler. My prayers during this two–year period became more questioning and complaining and seldom included meaningful prayers of praise or faith.

Once when I sat with Ford for one of his chemo treatments, I admired his child-like faith and smile. I responded with a smile, but inside I was furious at God. How could He let this happen to this young boy? I continued praying for healing, complaining and questioning quietly, and sometimes reminding God of His healing power. Here at age thirteen, Ford the cross-country runner was healed from ITP, his condition labeled as chronic, and there remained only a small chance of the disease appearing again. Praise God, the Great Healer.

Ford experienced some after effects from the disease and treatment. His hands and feet became slightly deformed, making it difficult for him to write clearly and to run with a normal pace. To help him adapt, he was able to use a computer for writing assignments, and he had special shoes that were supposed to train his feet as he developed. To compensate for his crooked feet, he began walking on his toes and developed a slightly unusual gait. It was difficult for him to run. As a young child, Ford loved to pretend play with his brothers and his friends. He always chose to play slow characters, a sloth, a turtle, or his favorite, the Komodo dragon. I never dreamed that Ford would run well, especially for long distances. Who would have imagined that he would choose to compete in a running sport? So, of course I overflowed with tears of joy at the cross-country meet on that September day.

Often the words *joy* and *happiness* are defined as synonyms, as if they could be used interchangeably. I believe the joy that has been infused into my life is so much more than happiness. In my definition, happiness is a feeling that depends upon circumstances, and joy is ours by faith *despite*

our circumstances. Often called the "joy" book,

Philippians is a part of the Bible that I have read over

and over again. Some of the verses, from the NIV,

that have influenced my joy journey are (with

emphases mine):

> I thank my God every time I remember
> you. In all my prayers for all of you, I
> always *pray with joy* because of your
> partnership in the gospel from the first
> day until now. (Philippians 1: 3–5)

> But even if I am being poured out like
> a drink offering on the sacrifice and
> service coming from your faith, I *am*
> *glad and rejoice with all of you.* So
> you too *should be glad and rejoice*
> *with me.* (Philippians 2: 17–18)

> Rejoice in the Lord always. I will say
> it again: Rejoice! Let your gentleness
> be evident to all. The Lord is near. Do
> not be anxious about anything, but in
> every situation, by prayer and petition,
> with thanksgiving, present your
> requests to God. And the peace of
> God, which transcends all
> understanding, will guard your hearts

and your minds in Christ Jesus.
(Philippians 4:4–7)

I rejoiced greatly in the Lord that at
last you renewed your concern for
me. Indeed, you were concerned, but
you had no opportunity to show it. I
am not saying this because I am in
need, for I have learned to be
content whatever the circumstances. I
know what it is to be in need, and I
know what it is to have plenty. I have
learned the secret of being content in
any and every situation, whether well
fed or hungry, whether living in plenty
or in want. *I can do all this through
him who gives me strength.*
(Philippians 4: 10–13)

And my God will meet all your
needs according to the riches of his
glory in Christ Jesus. (Philippians
4:18)

I am amazed at these statements in

Philippians, especially when I note that Paul wrote

them while he was a prisoner in Rome, chained to a

solder at his own expense. Imprisoned for two years,

he rejoices and encourages his readers to rejoice over

and over again *despite* his circumstances.

I am fortunate that even on rough days, I have found moments of joy that occur on a daily basis. A smile from someone I don't know, the sunshine over the snow-covered hills, baby birds learning to fly under the watch of their mother bird, the sunset over Lake Michigan, an encouraging word from my publisher, and the statement from a child who says, "I am so smart when you are here, Mrs. Copley!" Yes, I love those moments, they are joyful, and I try to go to sleep each night reviewing the joys I have experienced. Thankfully, joys are more than just moments.

Sometimes joy takes time to develop. Jerry was a colleague of mine at the University of Houston. When I first met him, he was the technology expert in my department, and we worked together on a variety of projects. He became aware that I was a Christian and had finished my undergraduate work at Olivet

Nazarene University. When I said that my daughter was going to go to Olivet as well, he emphatically stated that she should not go there because he had not had a good experience at another Nazarene university. I thanked him for his advice and we went on to other subjects.

Sixteen years later, Jerry and I were still at the university, but our roles had changed. I now served as the Chair of the Department of Curriculum and Instruction, and Jerry was the Director of Technology Services in the College of Education. One Friday night, I was working late in my office when Jerry and Mary, his new wife, appeared at the door. They wanted to talk to me about an exciting announcement. Mary was pregnant, and they were looking forward to their new addition. Then Jerry took a deep breath and asked if I could tell Mary about the Nazarene church because he wanted their child to be involved in a

Christian community. Surprised, I didn't ask him about his change of heart. Instead, I told both of them about my church and invited them to come to a Sunday service.

I met them the next Sunday morning, introduced them to our pastor, who had attended the same university as Jerry (isn't God amazing?), and they began attending Bible studies, as well as the regular services. Life was good, choosing joy was easy, and we were all excited to be part of their new journey as a family. And then their circumstances changed.

Jerry had been sick for a few weeks with what we thought was the flu. One afternoon I got a phone call from Mary. She asked me to come to the hospital because they had just admitted Jerry and were running a series of tests. Six months pregnant, Mary was worried. My secretary canceled my afternoon appointments, and another professor and I went to the hospital. Jerry was diagnosed with pancreatic cancer, and the prognosis was not good. In fact, they were not sure if Jerry would live long enough to see his baby born. It was difficult to be filled with joy that day, but I prayed with them and called our community to pray.

The next two years were filled with both joy and suffering. Jerry's health issues were difficult, but everyone watched as he trusted God with a joy and a peace that could not be easily explained. Jerry not only lived to see his daughter born, but he was able to dedicate her to God with Mary at his side. He got to play with his daughter, and some of my favorite memories of Jerry are of his laughter as he played all kinds of games with his joyful little girl. Both he and Mary got to experience the joys of a Christian community who cared for them with food, provisions, encouragements, and prayers that were amazing.

Jerry passed away on September 12, 2007, surrounded by his family and friends. His passing was peaceful, and his courage and strength made his leaving easier for everyone. A phrase from his obituary expressed his joy, "Jerry's days were not defined by his illness but were filled with the simple daily joys of his wife and daughter." I was honored to speak at his funeral, an uplifting celebration of his life and one that spoke to both the university and church communities.

I am fortunate to have shared the joys of others over the past forty years of my life, particularly the joy of giving to others. Because of God's providence and direction, I was given many opportunities to teach in different situations and to write math textbooks with talented authors, editors, publishers, and marketers. I was paid excellent salaries and royalties, more than I had dreamed. Chet and I had always paid our tithe, 10 percent of our income, as part of our commitment to God. Yet for the past forty years we have been privileged to give much more. I cannot adequately describe the overwhelming joy I have personally experienced by giving. Missions in Poland, Honduras, Argentina, Brazil, Bulgaria, and Kosovo, children sponsored in Bangladesh, the Jesus Film, endowed scholarships at Nazarene universities, and the library at Nazarene Theological Seminary received part of our gifts, and in turn we have been richly blessed and filled with joy.

Giving anonymous gifts to people we know has given us particular joy. We asked God and our pastors to help us see the needs of those around us and to help us give to them with no expectation of being paid back or thanked. It has been so much fun to surprise people with money that comes from God and to hear them rejoice in His provisions. Indeed, I can say with Paul, "And my God will meet all your needs according to the riches of his glory in Christ Jesus" (Philippians 4:19 NIV).

Chapter 9

A Journey through Grief

"Cancer free . . . and now Alzheimer's?"

Easter, April 21, 2019, was Chet's last Sunday at church. I had picked him up early from American House, a high-level Alzheimer's unit for the most advanced cases. The nurses had prepared him well, he was wearing my favorite shirt, his hair was combed, and his necessary medical equipment was properly hidden. His face was still bruised from his most recent fall, and he was confused about "why he had to use a walker to go to church." Our pastors were our daughter, Aimee, and son-in-law, Devin. Chet most often responded to music so Aimee had intentionally planned the service with Chet's favorite Easter song, "Because He Lives," and we all were hopeful that Chet would react to and maybe even sing with the congregation during that song. Unfortunately, Chet

133

was incapable of responding in any way. He was anxious and eager to get back to "his home." So he asked "the Big Boss," (my new name) to take him back there.

After I got him settled in his apartment, I cried all the way home and simply added another brick to my journey through grief, a journey I had begun six years earlier.

Chet retired at age sixty-two with all intentions of continuing his mission trips around the world. At the time his doctor was amazed at his health and the fact that he was not on any medication. A few months later, tests on a small mole on his arm resulted in a diagnosis of melanoma. At the doctor's office we received a description of the four levels of cancer, along with suggested treatments at each level. While we were waiting for the doctor, we read about all the levels and cheerfully surmised that at least we wouldn't be at level four, because the mole was so small, and the cancer couldn't possibly have spread.

After a long wait, the physician's assistant came in and simply said, "You have level four, melanoma skin cancer." If she said anything else, neither of us heard her. We had just read that if cancer is at level four, treatment was primarily palliative. We then met with the surgeon who examined his arm and told us how proficient he was at this type of surgery. We scheduled the date for the surgery, called friends and family, and began praying.

Over the next twelve years, Chet battled cancer. The surgery for melanoma was successful, and nothing spread to the lymph nodes. Then in a follow-up scan, cancer of the bladder was discovered. Again, Chet had surgery, and the tumor was successfully removed. A few years later, after many scans and biopsies, cancer was identified in the lining of his bladder, and a series of painful TB treatments were prescribed. During the months-long treatments, Chet developed serious eye infections and gout, along with enduring the continual biopsies and scans. Then an aggressive form of prostate cancer was detected, requiring twelve weeks of radiation treatments. Four kinds of cancer, six biopsies, two surgeries, one series of chemical treatments, one set of radiation treatments, lots of prayer, and a series of caring health care providers became part of our lives. Although Chet continued to have scans and six-month check-ups, we heard the words, "cancer-free . . . at least for now" in February of 2014. We were thrilled!

The twelve years of cancer, scans, and biopsies taught us so much. We learned that we could face this together with God's help. We both wanted to continue our life of travel, Chet's mission work, and my work in the math world. We discovered that our lives did not need to change much. We just needed to schedule treatments around cancer issues. Chet seldom complained, and I kept myself busy making schedules, rescheduling trips when Chet was too ill, getting us to the treatments on time, and following the doctors' orders.

We had wonderful support from both family and friends. Aimee and Devin and our new grandsons provided so much joy, and we often visited them or they visited us. My sisters, brother, mother, and step-dad covered us with prayers and included times with Chet at the hospital and home. Our Sunday school class and our church members prayed for us and demonstrated both sympathy and empathy for us. During our cancer journey, ten of our closest friends had different kinds of cancer, all types of treatment, all types of supporting relationships, and a variety of diagnoses from chronic to life-threatening. We continued to enjoy our life, shared our cancer stories with others, celebrated every time we finished a treatment or heard encouraging words, and often spent time with our friends, laughing about the interesting side effects of treatments.

We both made new friends during the treatments. Chet teased his health and treatment providers and often left them laughing. I enjoyed talking and often crying with the other caregivers while we waited for each of the treatments to be completed. Through it all, we learned that our lives were in God's hands, and our hope in Him seldom wavered.

Our journey changed during the summer of 2014. We were traveling across Germany and England with friends from the Nazarene Seminary in Kansas City. Chet had great difficulty keeping up with everyone, remembering where we were, and his normal happy attitude seemed to disappear. I thought it was the result of "cancer brain" and continued to explain to others and myself that he was cancer-free and he was just tired. When we arrived home, he went through a series of tests for five hours at a hospital in Houston. The diagnosis was "99 percent sure that Chet has Alzheimer's." My journey through grief began.

In the early days of Alzheimer's, I learned so much about myself and Chet's love for me and others. We were traveling on a short flight from Chicago to Muskegon, and we were assigned different seats. I was dismayed when I saw the person next to my husband and labeled her "Tattoo Woman." She was covered with tattoos from head to toe, had a large variety of piercings, and wore jeans with many holes. I watched as my husband talked non-stop to her during the entire trip. I knew my husband's aversion to tattoos and body piercings, and I was worried that his new filter-less conversation could present some problems. I prayed that the thirty-minute flight would be over soon.

When we arrived, both my husband and Tattoo Woman were still talking, and they both looked happy. When I asked my husband what they had talked about, naturally, he couldn't remember. I was relieved and felt glad that we would never meet Tattoo Woman again. But God had a different plan.

As we checked in for the return flight the next week, I turned around and heard Tattoo Woman greet my husband. I sighed and we quickly boarded the plane. Again, we were in different rows, but this time I was the one seated next to Tattoo Woman. As soon as she sat down, she turned to me and exclaimed, "Oh, you are the wonderful lady that has been married for more than thirty years. I really need to talk to you! How in the world do you find a man who can make you happy?" So, for the next thirty minutes, I told her how God was the center of our lives together and the importance of Christian relationships. By God's providential grace, the lesson that I had just studied was about the Samaritan woman (John 4) and as Tattoo Woman shared her life of many broken relationships, I was able to tell her the beautiful story of a woman who had met the Savior. We prayed together, and when the thirty-minute trip was completed, we parted ways—both of us different people.

Over the next six years, I lost my beloved Chet bit by bit. I spent much of the first year devouring every piece of information I could, reading more than fifteen books about Alzheimer's, analyzing the effectiveness of medications and treatments, and helping Chet remember important information through all of my previously effective teaching practices. After all, we had conquered cancer, so we could handle this diagnosis as well. I did not see myself as a good caregiver, and during this first year I reminded God of that fact. I just knew that God would help us and a miracle would occur.

But we did not get a miracle. The disease continued to progress. The man who always knew where he was got lost finding his way home. The man who could remember everyone he had ever met couldn't recall anyone's name without prompting. The man who always told the truth now created the most amazing stories about his daily activities, none of which were true. The man who remembered everything he had ever read couldn't correctly identify the year he was born or who the president was. The man who loved playing with his grandsons was often bothered by their noise. The man who was always kind to others began to say everything he thought in a very tactless manner. The man who loved to travel and work around the house only wanted to sit in his chair and issue orders for service. The man who showered everyday and was often categorized as a neat freak avoided all personal hygiene activities. I grieved the loss of the man I knew as Chet Copley.

Some of the effects of Alzheimer's were humorous. Chet hid my wrapped Christmas present that Aimee and he had purchased for me, and we found it a week later wrapped in a pair of his underwear. Chet informed the rather large lady sitting next to him at our grandson's school concert that if she were smaller, it would be easier to sit next to her. Chet told everyone he met that he had been in more than a hundred countries in his life, a number that increased each time he said it. Chet explained to the doctor that Teddy Roosevelt was the current president and that all he remembered about him was that he didn't like him. Chet ate twenty Oreo cookies from the pantry in one hour and then blamed our son-in-law for their disappearance. Chet frequently told everyone how to drive, giving specific directions that were usually the opposite of what they should be doing. Chet reported amazing physical feats like running all the way around Lake Michigan before lunch or climbing trees or re-shingling the roof. Chet and a fellow patient tried to break out from a daycare facility using their walkers, an effort that didn't work no matter how many times they tried. Despite moments of humor, I grieved the loss of my husband's rational mind.

As the disease progressed, the effects of Alzheimer's were anything but humorous. Chet reluctantly gave his precious truck to our son-in-law because he could no longer drive it. We bought a special chair because he couldn't sleep in a bed due to his fears of not being able to breath. We put special equipment throughout the house, including grab bars and a walk-in tub. Still he fell often, became bruised, and had difficulty moving from place to place. When he developed scar tissue from the cancer treatments, he had to permanently wear a bag, a situation that he did not understand. He continually tried to remedy the situation by physically pulling out the tubes, resulting in frequent accidents. As these events multiplied, my grief increased, I became more and more frustrated at my inadequacy as a caregiver, and I began to realize that I was not only losing Chet. I was losing me.

My immediate family offered support and made rather forceful suggestions. Thankfully, Aimee was especially assertive. Initially, she insisted we find some type of daycare so that I could have some time during the day to myself. She also helped me evaluate the private nurses we hired, and when our home became more and more hospital-like, she joined me as we visited the nursing home that had the best references. At that first visit I was in the middle of explaining to the director that I was just "thinking about" placing Chet in a home "in the future" when Aimee arrived. She simply said to both of us, "It is time today. My dad needs to be here. Can you show us an apartment?" The director smiled and immediately showed us a beautiful apartment that was perfect for Chet. We moved him later in the week, and while I continued grieving for the loss of Chet, I was able to begin creating a new life for me. My cousin, a hospital director, encouraged me and helped me to speak the truth that I wanted to change my role from caregiver to my original role as wife. I visited Chet almost every day, made sure that his care was excellent, cried and grieved all the way home, and then spent the rest of the time working, playing, praying, and refocusing my life to include my needs and health.

Chet passed away three and a half months after he moved to American House. When I arrived Tuesday morning, June 25, 2019, I found him being ministered to by his gifted nurses. He was not responsive. When Aimee arrived, the hospice nurse, Aimee, and I surrounded his chair, prayed, and sang all of his favorite hymns. It was a beautiful hour, and I have no doubt that God's presence filled the room. Aimee's powerful voice was Chet's favorite, and I know that heaven and all the residents of the home heard every word. Chet's only response was to the words of "It is Well." As Aimee sang, he raised his arm slightly and pointed to heaven. We all knew what he meant.

God gave me a very special gift a few hours later. The nurses all left with promises and directions for any help I needed. Aimee went to find some food for us because we hadn't eaten all day. Chet appeared to be sleeping, and I held his hand. It was just Chet, God, and I. I told him how much I loved him. I watched and listened as he coughed and then left on his heavenward journey. Through tear-stained eyes, I realized that he was gone and that his physical body was just a shell. Chet Copley was not there. At that moment, I was the only person on earth who knew Chet was with God. I sat there for a few minutes, praising God for inviting him to be in heavenly places. I was at peace, and I knew Chet was as well.

We celebrated Chet's life in three different places. When Chet was first diagnosed with cancer, we had discussed the type of funeral we would want, so I already knew what he desired. We had a funeral in Michigan where we had lived for five years. Our son-in-law pastor Devin officiated, Aimee sang, and different family members spoke. Our Michigan church family only knew the Alzheimer's Chet, and they loved him. I was amazed at the number of people who told me how Chet had influenced them with his gentle spirit. Then we returned to Houston, where we had lived and served for more than thirty years, for another funeral. These were people who knew the *not* Alzheimer's Chet, and I thoroughly enjoyed the many memories they shared. Finally, we had a graveside service in Illinois, where Chet's ashes were buried in the Copley plot with his three brothers, mother, and father. These celebrations of Chet's life were especially meaningful to me. I needed to be reminded of beautiful memories of the healthy Chet. I needed to hear stories of Chet's influence. I needed to see how many people loved him. And most important, I needed to share my conviction that Chet was with

God and that I would see him again.

On April 12, 2020, I celebrated Easter without

Chet. It was a difficult, yet satisfying, Sunday. And I

sang,

> Because He lives, I can face tomorrow,
> Because He lives, all fear is gone,
> Because I know He holds the future,
> Life is worth the living just because He lives. [i]

Yes, I am still going through my grieving journey, and I will never forget the thirty-six years I had with Chet Copley. I will always miss him, but I know that "because Jesus lives," my life continues to be worth the living.

Chapter 10

A Journey of Faith

"The Lord is my shepherd?"

One afternoon in late February, I asked my five-year-old grandson how his school day had been.

Ford sighed. "I am *so* tired. We have had to count to one hundred *all* day, over and over again!"

As a former kindergarten teacher, I recognized his partially eaten Cheerio necklace as a symbol celebrating the hundredth day of school. Ah, a teaching opportunity. Being a math teacher, I found a one hundred chart in my bag and showed him the square representation of the numbers one to one hundred. I proceeded to ask him to find the number that showed his age and the ages of his parents, brothers, and grandparents.

When he found Papa's age, he declared, "Papa, you are almost at the end!" Later he wondered, "Did Papa start at one?"

I resonate with Ford's words, "the end," as I write this last chapter describing my journey of faith. The coronavirus outbreak of 2020 and my "elderly" status were reiterated over and over by people encouraging me to take necessary precautions to stay safe and healthy. While I did not get ill, the pandemic certainly made me think more about my age and how vulnerable I can be. Even without a physical problem, there certainly are days that I feel old, especially after times of challenge or stress.

From the beginning of my life until now, my journey of faith has been transformed. As a young child, my faith in God equated to my family, particularly my dad. As I grew older, my faith in God was blended with my faith in education, in my husband's love, in specific organizations, in America, in justice, in financial security, in my immediate or extended family, or in strong friendships. Now, after some disappointing experiences, I am learning to put my total faith in God. Without a doubt in my mind, He has never failed me and He never will.

The twenty-third Psalm is my faith scripture. I memorized all five verses from the King James Version at age eight because I wanted to win a contest. I was the first child to accurately repeat it to Mrs. Essex, my Bible teacher. I am sure that I had little understanding of the meaning of Psalm 23 at that time. However, over the years, my understanding of each verse has increased, and even now, more than sixty years later and as often happens with Scripture, I continue to glean new meanings of this famous psalm and the shepherd-sheep metaphor.

The LORD is my shepherd;

I shall not want.

The Lord is *my* shepherd. Just as a shepherd looks after his sheep with total dedication, *my* shepherd is a personal caregiver. I have often been asked if God cares about the everyday events of my life. I believe He does, just as the shepherd cares for his sheep. He knows my name and everything about me. More importantly, He makes sure I have everything I need. Over and over again, God has provided for my financial needs, my physical needs, my emotional needs, my security needs, and most important, my need to be loved.

One time my financial need was especially great. After Chet was diagnosed with Alzheimer's, I met with several lawyers, as well as home care specialists. Although we had saved money for our retirement, the amount of money required for Chet's future care appeared to be astronomical, and because

of our savings, we would be totally responsible for his
care. In fact, one lawyer suggested that if we got a
divorce, it would be "helpful to your finances" or that
I now needed to "quit giving and provide for my
husband." God helped me find a Christian lawyer,
and as always, God made a way for me to provide a
beautiful and caring environment for Chet, financial
security for me, and still allowed me to experience the
joy of giving. I praise God!

> He maketh me to lie down in green pastures:
> he leadeth me beside the still waters.

I have learned that sheep will not lie down
unless they are free from all fear, specifically, fear of
predators, free from friction with other sheep, free
from pests, and free from fear of not finding food.
Shepherds must actually *make* sheep lie down. Also, a
shepherd has to *lead* his sheep to the good water
because without his direction, they will drink stagnant

157

or unhealthy nourishment. Often the good water is in a difficult place, and the shepherd necessarily must build a path to refreshing water.

Again, this metaphor applies to my life. I have some rather silly fears. Chet often teased me that I was the official door checker in our home. Every night before we went to bed, I would check all the doors to make sure they were locked, make sure the outdoor lights were on, and set the house alarm. Now that I am by myself, I still follow the same procedure; however, for a few months after Chet passed, my door-checking procedures were not quite the same. I began checking the doors more than once a night, and I would obsessively get out of bed and re-check them several times. Lying in bed, I heard every noise--all the haunting sirens, outside voices, and even falling tree limbs. Or I would visualize all the things that could possibly occur at night when I had no human protection or light. It may sound irrational. Now I am

thankful that God has provided the peace, the green

pastures, and the still water so I can sleep and live

without fear.

> He restoreth my soul:
> he leadeth me in the paths of righteousness
> for his name's sake.

This verse really applies to me. As described

in almost every chapter in this book, I am obsessively

goal-oriented. I often overwork and overschedule

others and myself. I can name many times when God

has restored my soul and caused me to rest in Him. I

can also say with certainty that God frequently tells

me to be still and acknowledge that He is God and

that situations are in His control. God always listens

to me when I pray, counsels me every time I need

direction, and even when I don't ask for His direction,

He shows me the right things to do.

In one specific situation, I heard God's voice almost audibly. I was a physically mature, naïve, and socially insecure seventh grader in a new school. Because of my ability to be first chair flutist in the band, I was asked to go to the high school and be involved in advanced band activities. There I met an older boy who was interested in being my boyfriend. His relationship ideas were very different than mine, and God protected me from a sexual abuse situation with the words, "Get out of here!" I never saw the boy again. I also never told anyone about it until fifty years later. But that day I know I heard and followed God's direction.

Yea, though I walk through the valley of the shadow
of death,
I will fear no evil: for thou art with me;
thy rod and thy staff they comfort me.

God is with me no matter what the situation is. Hallelujah! Sometimes I see His presence in an overwhelming way; I know He is there, and I feel Him and hear His voice through Scripture or prayer. Other times I wonder where He is, and yet I affirm mentally and emotionally that He is with me always. I have always hated the term *blind* faith. As a researcher who analyzed data regarding learning, I have often made predictions about future education techniques based on past performances. My faith in God is not blind. Instead, similar to my research procedures, my eyes are wide open to my past experiences as I analyze how God has provided love, guidance, and mercy throughout my life. I can say without reservation that His rod and staff provide the love and discipline that keeps me safe, and His protection gives me comfort in all situations.

> Thou preparest a table before me
> in the presence of mine enemies:
> thou anointest my head with oil;
> my cup runneth over.

In Rabbi Pesach Wolicki's discussion of the Hebrew meaning of this strange verse, from verse 4 to 5, he surmises that David changed from the sheep image to a human image, one created in the image of God. He said, "We battle our enemies. We defeat them with the help and strength and confidence that God provides for us. He empowers us and gives us responsibility. He sets the table. He fills the cup. He gives us anointing, strength, and confidence."[i] I love this idea!

As a Christian who lives and works in the world, my beliefs about God and other subjects have often been questioned or critiqued. How do you know God really cares? Why are you giving to missions? Isn't that a waste of your money? Do you really believe that change can happen in that situation? Why doesn't God do _____? Would a loving God let _____ happen? Religion is just for people who need a crutch. I don't believe in prayer, so don't pray for me. These words are just a few that I have heard during my journey. I know that God has provided and will continue to provide the strength and confidence to share my faith with His words and Spirit.

Surely goodness and mercy shall follow me
all the days of my life:
and I will dwell in the house of the LORD forever.

Stated simply, God's goodness and forgiveness will always be with me. There is nothing I can do to merit more of His love and mercy, and there is nothing I can do that will merit less of His love and mercy. How exciting! I need only accept His love, ask for His forgiveness, and I will abide with Him. What a wonderful promise and one that I know will be kept forever.

One time, Chet and I were traveling with Aimee and Devin and the boys. As we were going to our hotel rooms, I tripped over the stairs and fell face-first on the floor. I was briefly winded and did not immediately move. When I opened my eyes, Ford was on his knees, looking directly at me. He asked, "Are you going to heaven now, Meme?" I smiled, sat up slowly and said, "Not now because I am needed here, but someday."

As I think about my future, I look forward to what God has in store for me to do. I am still working on math books, and I still share teaching experiences and suggestions with teachers and students. Most recently, I have enjoyed speaking and planning retreats for women, Bible schools for children, and learning activities for my grandsons. In many ways I am not done yet.

I close this chapter and this book with the words of a song that describes my faith journey. In 1923, Thomas Chisholm penned these words to describe God's faithfulness. Many years later, they

still express my journey of faith in a God who is

always faithful.

> Great is Thy faithfulness, O God my Father!
> There is no shadow of turning with Thee;
> Thou changest not, Thy compassions, they fail
> not
> As Thou has been, Thou forever wilt be.
>
> Great is Thy faithfulness.
> Morning by morning new mercies I see;
> All I have needed thy hand hath provided.
> Great is Thy faithfulness, Lord unto me!
>
> Summer and winter, and springtime and
> harvest,
> Sun, moon, and stars in their courses above.
> Join with all nature in manifold witness
> To Thy great faithfulness, mercy, and love.
>
> Pardon for sin and a peace that endureth,
> Thine own dear presence to cheer and to
> guide,
> Strength for today and bright hope for
> tomorrow
> Blessings all mine, with ten thousand beside[ii]

Endnotes

[i]Public Domain
[ii]Brennan Manning, *The Wisdom of Tenderness,* HarperOne Publishers, 2002.

Chapter 1: The Beginning
[i]Brene Brown, *The Gifts of Imperfection*, Hazelden Publishing, 2010.

Chapter 9: My Journey through Grief
[i]Bill and Gloria Gaither, "Because He Lives," Spring House, 1998.

Chapter 10: My Journey of Faith
[i]https://theisraelbible.com/psalm-235-since-when-do-sheep-sit-at-a-table/
[ii]Public Domain

About the Author

Juanita Copley is a Professor Emerita from the University of Houston, where she taught mathematics education courses. She continues to teach Bible studies, public school teachers, ladies' retreat participants, children's Bible schools, and most importantly her three grandsons during "Meme's Summer School." She has authored a variety of mathematics books for teachers and students.

Made in the USA
Columbia, SC
30 December 2020